Afterlives

Christopher Palmer

Afterlives

Acknowledgements

My thanks are due to the editors of the following publications, in which many of these poems first appeared, some in earlier versions: *ACTWrite*, *a fine line* (NZ), *The Age*, *Ask the Rain* (Poets Union Inc. anthology 2004), *Australian Poetry Journal*, *Blue Dog: Australian Poetry*, *Burley*, *Canberra City News*, *The Canberra Times*, *Centralian Advocate*, *Communion Literary Magazine*, *Famous Reporter*, *Five Bells*, *Meanjin*, *Quadrant*, *Social Alternatives*, *Sotto*, *The Sydney Morning Herald*, *The Victorian Naturalist* and *The Weekend Australian*.

'On the death of the past' was shortlisted for the 2015 Dorothy Porter Prize for Poetry.

'Capital cities' was the winner of the 2002 ACT Writers Centre Poetry Award.

Sincere thanks are due to Stephen Matthews at Ginninderra Press for his support of first-time authors and his patience and diligence in the preparation of the manuscript.

Several of these poems benefited from the early critical insight of Geoff Page; and from that of Leesa, always the first sounding board.

For J and L

Afterlives
ISBN 978 1 74027 165 7
Copyright © Christopher Palmer 2016
Cover: *Going home* (detail), by Tom Roberts, oil, ca 1889, National Gallery of Australia, Canberra

First published 2016 by
GINNINDERRA PRESS
PO Box 3461 Port Adelaide 5015 Australia
www.ginninderrapress.com.au

Contents

Passenger flight	9
Woman on the bus	11
Voyeur	12
Reflections	13
Six pinches of time	14
The most of you	15
Love affair	16
The god of tiny things	17
Happenings	18
Protectors of the fairy garden	20
Ligature	21
( )	22
Epitaph	23
People and clocks	24
Sonnet #7	25
In my mother's country	26
A western shade of red	27
Extract from a record of an expedition…	29
At Emily Gap	32
Lucy	33
Naturam primum cognoscere rerum	34
Gallipoli, dawn	35
Convicts sentenced at Norfolk Island & Port Arthur	36
A life in the Ardennes	37
Condemned	38
Echo	39
On the death of the past	40
An equation and a final solution	41
Forensics	42
Unnatural histories	43

Chromosome	44
Form and function	45
To *Aliceathrips palmeri*	46
Growing notes for banksias	47
The poplar effect	50
Mayfly	52
Nomenclature	53
Weeding	54
Meanwhile, at Floriade…	55
Monday, 8 a.m.	57
A lesson in servitude	58
Capital cities	59
At the corner store	60
William Carlos Williams	61
Thank you for your submission	62
Untitled	63
Notes	64

feeling you gently
shaking my arm, I awoke
and found you asleep

Passenger flight

I've studied them, and know them all.
I know them all by name.
There's the one who walks with his head bowed; the one
who glances behind at a source of paranoia I can't see;
the one whose beauty always captivates at first sight
before quickly falling away.

                       Here comes the woman
who's never been considered a workaholic;
who dreams every kind of dream.
She always says she won't be back on Monday
after winning the weekend lottery,
but never does.

                       That man over there
likes to read graffiti and people's tattoos.
He likes alleyways and looking behind facades;
believes that every posed photo is a fake.

                       Behind him is the academic
who reads scientific papers all the way home.
As soon as he gets inside he closes the door to his study
and masturbates while looking at his resumé.

                       Across the aisle
is the woman who lives her life in the cinema.
She imagines us all as the cast of her latest movie;
the greatest actor to wear flannelette haute couture.
Out of all the people she's met in her life
she wonders how many think of her now.

>   Then there's the man
> who sometimes sits in my seat. He says hello
> with just the right amount of distance,
> wills others into sitting elsewhere. His song begins
> as he reaches his desk each morning.
>   What forces
> create this loose community every day…
> a group that forms and breaks out of circumstance;
> not quite together and never the same each journey
>   – the soft shape of a cloud –
> our lives carried in our bags and on our faces,
>   reflected in the glass
> travelling inside ourselves
> extras in each other's films.

Woman on the bus

Waiting, I look to see if she's there as we approach
sit more upright in my seat. She doesn't always get on
but today she fills my eyes and mind again.
Sitting in her usual space near the driver,
she only travels a short distance.
Wearing black, accentuating her hair
she ties it up to expose the nape of her neck
and I'm sixteen years old.
Some days I wonder what her voice sounds like
what her name might be. On dull days
her reflection lingers in the glass.
Seeing her for a few minutes each time
slowly painting my picture. Even if I didn't work
I'd still need to catch this bus.

Voyeur

I perve, sometimes, at your nostrils;
the way they are upturned, like palms;
a pair of adjectives that describe your face.

But they're not the same:
each ellipse is tilted slightly differently
on its own axis, and their divide

is the spring-source for the scar
which underlines the left edge of your philtrum –
from the Greek *philtron*, meaning love potion.

I look, feeding when your eyes glance away,
closing my own to paint and then store
the outline of your nose for nourishment

when you're not here;
how it follows its easy trajectory
and skims the surface of your face

leading to your carefully placed, volatile lips:
a noose for all that is unsaid.

Reflections

I like studying the Nazca Lines
You like studying the lines on Samuel Beckett's face

I like reading only the first and last paragraphs of book reviews
You like reading only the books themselves

I like to wonder at the internal workings of mirrors
You like wondering how many people have never known
                                          what they look like

I like those moments of mutual physical attraction
You like to feel the attraction here, and here

*

You like people that like themselves
I like people that know themselves

You like watching people
I like looking at people looking at you

You like to say I sound like my son
I like convincing him that it's 'zed' and not 'zee'

You like the dimples on my face and what they say to you
I like the dimples on your lower back and what they say to me

Six pinches of time

evensong:
the cicada's drum
of your heart

*

the birds are getting edgy –
your thoughts take to the air

*

outside
the crow sings
your absence

*

strangers turn their heads
to have their fix of you

*

darkness at noon –
the sun in your shadow

*

tonight the salve
of your moth-soft skin

The most of you

Brief acknowledgement
of morning, then talk like we
rhyme, or else the world
in free verse, until evening.
But we never say goodnight.

Love affair

She's multiplied by the sum of her parts;
qualities that attracted me to her
in the first place. Tall and reflective,

she still has her narrow waist despite the years.
This was how it began,
and just like then it starts with her still.

When turned on she sings an aria
while creating dark nectar
from simple raw materials.

She's fickle, turning off
as quickly as being turned on,
but by then her creation is complete:

golden velvet above a serene, black lake.
I begin to drink the aroma
before inhaling the liquid, at the same time

realising how easily life's difficulties
are extinguished by this solution
to a simple equation that is held in my hand.

The god of tiny things

inhabits maybes
fills his eyes with me

softens the dawn
with his fine white down

chirrups and chirps
like a cricketer

knows the world
is bigger than the word

*

Upside down, waiting for his show to begin.
Koala-like, hugging the arm of a chair.

Balancing on the crook formed by my foot and shin.
Wearing his favourite colour, like some red-carpet premiere.

Standing on the couch, clapping his favourite villain.
Thumb in mouth, other hand curling hair.

A lizard on the floor, propping up a chin.
Sitting, quietly, with a mannequin's stare.

Happenings

I saw his six-week-old heart
blinking at me through soft tissue and a hard drive.
Almost nine months later
he's wrapped in a towel, looking up –
he knows who I am.

*

He's developing a sense of humour
even before he's talking:
a sideways glance followed by a smile
repeated twenty times.

*

I surprise him in his bedroom
with a truck and some cars.
'I'm not really playing,
I'm pretending to play,' he says

*

He tells me he's going to kill a fly
with a coffee plunger.
I wish him luck,
glad to have just finished my long black.
Within five minutes he returns
with a murder weapon
and a body.

*

Aged 5½ he receives the first wound from his adventures
that will scar; the end of the skin given to him.
But I want to focus on his natural topography
and the tiny depression on his midriff he was born with,
my landmark.

       *

Sometimes I watch him, unnoticed
wondering if I know who he is.
Today I explain how fossils are formed
how the area was once a sea bed
and he immediately repeats my explanation
      back to me.
Now one life form looks on another
separated by two hundred million years,
              unaware
we're making his own distant past.

Protectors of the fairy garden

Don't stray from the path; it isn't a stroll.
Move closer and listen. I'll be the scout.
Come on, keep up, this is a troll patrol.

Avoid their gaze or they will steal your soul.
Under the fig tree's where they hang out.
Don't stray from the path; it isn't a stroll.

Check the woodpile, and the cubbyhole.
Just when we thought there was nothing about.
Come on, keep up, this is a troll patrol.

Close your eyes and they will eat you whole.
Remember to whisper, never shout.
Don't stray from the path; it isn't a stroll.

Answer their questions and you'll pay a toll.
They thrive and breed if they sense any doubt.
Come on, keep up, this is a troll patrol.

Be watchful, look sharp. Stay in control.
If you're cornered, aim for a knockout.
Don't stray from the path; it isn't a stroll.
Come on, keep up. This is a troll patrol.

Ligature

She sits on the bench
devouring the flesh
of the unpicked olive.

Abandoned by Artemis
her expectations lie scattered
in front of her, and she watches

as each is gobbled up by birds
which have congregated,
expectantly.

She knows how they care for their young
that the paternal bond can be so strong
and what happens to the ones

that aren't looked after.
She notices those most of all
gaping in a constant hunger

while her own grows fat
on a diet of constant irritation
to the milky sap

of the fig.
Perhaps today she'll obey
the aching voice

that drifts down
from the escarpment
enveloping her every time

they visit the park.
A voice that says
leave him behind.

(   )

& here you are again   a don't wannabe bogun
reminding me of my place in the world   *i heard*
you went travelling i say   breathing old air
back when tanzania was pronounced like tasmania
& benelux was a washing powder   you say
you've just done south-east asia   that i liked to travel
& i did   but had to drag you to the moon
        so you have eyes the colour of gravity & skin
that drugged me in the hours before dawn   yes
you saw the beauty in people but your own body
offended you & you had to be reassured that
asymmetry really is sexy   and now   on the eve
of your epic pageant   you go in one eye
and out the other
        how's your hair been i ask   but you sidestep
cleverly   saying you gave up cigarettes
but took up facebook   how you only visit the mall
for the extreme parking
        you once said that science is all plants and particles
& talked of the real world   when i remarked on the
destructive potential of meteorites   you replied
you needed new slippers
        how your whispers came to hold such violence
enough   perhaps   to fill an empty poem
you ask what we were once   (   ) i say

Epitaph

Together
you are *Mary Celeste* and *Mary Rose*
dissolved of all bonds   deeper than
anyone could think   translating a cathode
ray tube   or else a pinhole camera
where everything is upside down.
Yes, your reich spans four walls.

Together
you were the larva of my life
in polyphonic surround sound   existing in
all dimensions   sometimes white dwarf
sometimes black hole   always zero gravity
collapsed at the very end point of light.
Yes, vitriol is my television.

People and clocks

One is an exhibitionist, the other a voyeur.
    Clocks have only limited numerical skills.
For every person in the world there are 4.6 clocks.
    Both function in the 'now'.
A clock does very little with three hands.
    Both obey the laws of mechanics.
People think, erroneously, they can save time.
    A clock doesn't change its behaviour when watched.
Both bear the signature of a maker.
    The faces of some people are easier to read.

Sonnet #7

Through the previous eighty years of coming last
in the corner, leaning into its past
of being rubbed, ochred, and rubbed again
to remind of when the earth admired men.
The faded yellow bands, the marks, the grooves
that run its length. Used where nothing moves;
those that felt its edge, or blackened its tip
or raised it in ceremony or kinship.
A silent 'L', and yet, above the noise
I stroke its curve, listening for a voice.
You can have it for eighty he says
sure of a sale. Its story greys.
Across the shelves and ornaments something drips
as I wipe the dust from my fingertips.

In my mother's country

I am here
to discover facts
that are already known
and to name things
that already have names
like *Hyles livornicoides*
for the *ayepe-arenye*.
I am a translator
living in an expanding technicality.

A western shade of red

i

Now in dead hands
your architecture speaks of fortitude
while the middle-age spread of your legs opens wide
my eyes to this church for the part time pilgrims
and the petty fondling of gosse   horn   cobb and co
saluting our very own aussiemandias
expecting nothing but the well heeled   the high heeled
and the weather   dissecting your loading zones
knowing your joints   your fossils
rotting away the cambrian
rendering your fat as quickly
as they invent it.
You're as immoveable
as a liar's truths.

ii

Exposed to nothing
but the gentle lapping of the sand
and all the lovely suns
the McHappy customers use you as a roundabout
to see your visages and mirages
going straight to the top floor
as sirens wail below
their plastic mountain that they find
to cut out and keep
where nothing is sacred
and all the world's an ice cream
delaying the small matter of your turning
to a long truce
whispered in Alice's ear
so that all there was to live has been lived
but these are slippery times
learn to turn away
make a wreck of them
for only you can save this world.

Extract from a record of an expedition through central Australia

7 Nov

The sun ignores the shirts on our backs
    and the wind compresses us so that we shrink away.
We have walked this country, filling up on its emptiness:
    of nevergreen trees and their shady suggestions,
rivers whose only current is the steady flow
    of disappointment, and eddies of sand
that make us long for the integument of an insect.
    The air is muddy with flies; they erode our calm.
What blacks we've seen are fairly covered with them:
    they squint their eyes and mouths to keep them out
and they being so troublesome we have become
    just so many blinking creatures ourselves.
In order to keep entire possession of our senses
    we must employ the assistance of both hands.
And still they beat us and they beat us still.

25 Nov

The rift between my mind and madness has narrowed
    since we entered the spinifex.
Oh, how I curse its crusade!
    It probes and pikes and punctures in sheaves
until all wear its tussocky uniform.
    The plant has a peculiar habit of dying from the inside out
as though to secure its future it must surrender its past.
    If I could somehow not play with my wife's hair
or sip tea from porcelain cups
    I might also learn to live this way.

20 Dec

The landscape is heir to the day's last, redemptive gift.
    I have found the inland sea so desperately sought and longed-for:
the plains are by turns saturated in honeycomb
    a shade of pink found nowhere else
and red so everywhere it must be fake
    so that all my thoughts are flooded with verse.
This intense scenery is within me
    creating a reality from which I cannot avert my eyes.

27 Dec

Up early, already bearing the sky's vast tonnage.
    Parsons counted the last of our stores:
six bags of flour, three bags of sugar
    three of tea and seven gallons of water
all to last until we reach the depot;
    a treasury that lies always just beyond those trees.
We also have the camels, and their demise
    would mean no longer listening to their miserable soundtrack.
In the time it takes to manipulate the contents of an empty box
    I conducted an inventory of myself, finding I am lacking surety
as well as sufficient purchase on my character.
    And yet from the quickest perusal of my hands
it is plain that a man can hold two futures.

11 Feb

We turned north, following the smokes
        and were found, lapping at vowels
clutching our promises
        waiting to be released into the sand.
They appeared to us like clouds
        while we wondered where in history
fate would place us.

19 Mar

What we are looking for I am beginning to understand
        and what began as exploration has become a search for authenticity
where once we would have crushed its massive bones.
        They call us *alatja* which Yimpi said means
'those who have only just arrived'.
        The natives inhabit a different country; they walk its streets
understanding every intonation of its text.
        I too read the land, as I do our maps
and the journals of our peers
        but learn no facts.
I have travelled into the distance and to another place
        yet I must pull away
lest I be carried too far from home…

At Emily Gap

    I came from my *altyerrenge*
to be inundated by another narrative
                        where the ranges are a kind of text
      and animals are people.
          Sacred tracks of the caterpillar women
      point towards the sky
                     while a low bird
gets caught in the silence.
      Near the entrance
          a woman kicks up the sand
      lights up a smoke
          and asks how much a mountain weighs.
Gillen's dreamtime is just a dream.

Lucy

member of the Laetolil Ladies Club
Olduvai Old School
united by a rift
and known from Afar
by her homo descendants

Naturam primum cognoscere rerum

I had always admired their careful paring of layers
removing the strands year by year
      around some iron age figure
until he lay   utterly undone
                      brought back
to beyond what he was.
I marvelled at how the dead could be so clean
      wearing nothing but a number
as a stranger in a lab coat
welcomed him to the new world
temperature-controlled and fluorescent
before exhibiting him under glass.
And now I fall towards what long ago
      trickled away in the melt water
to somewhere behind his eyes
and wonder for how long must the dead be
before it's acceptable to unearth them;
who out of us will be dug up
      and prepared for display.

Gallipoli, dawn

The moon drills long lines in the hillside.
Thousands stand like crosses, swaddled in their flag,
fatigued into stillness. Each has his private war,
and an inherited love of country
undiminished in the rush towards death.
Roused by speeches of valour and honour
they don't talk of why, but of where and how
until a lone bugler finishes what they're unable to say.
Those loitering at the pie stand wipe ketchup
from their hands; some buy a souvenir,
while others blush as the occasion
builds within them, the issue perfectly formed,
something that a night full of liquor can't dull.
And then the fighting starts.

Convicts sentenced at Norfolk Island & Port Arthur Tasmania

William Mansfield	30 September 1851	Wilfully tearing his towel	14 days solitary confinement
	6 December 1852	Having some bread improperly	2 months hard labour in chains
Edward Coombs	18 September 1846	Absent without leave and having snares and some pudding in his possession	6 months hard labour in chains
	24 September 1851	Piratically seizing a boat	Fully committed for trial
George Britton	3 July 1837	Not giving his shirt to be washed	18 hours solitary confinement on bread and water
	16 August 1847	Attempting to carry a library book into the church	2 months in chains

A life in the Ardennes

is lived in a dulled nature
without breathing in the humus
or feeling the finely honed nip of pine needles.
It is lived between interlocking limbs
where time is measured in inches and feet
and by the steady flow of replacements.

No longer the low open fields of the midwest
which now occupy the higher ridges
of my memory.
Instead, I am surrendered to a present
dominated by the timidity of our intellects
where the night is a slow beginning
and the dawn a sudden end.

Winter falls every day,
defining our pocket horizons, and completing
the fragile circle of our progress.
Occasionally I find myself still alive:
a sudden flower, cracks in the sky
that reveal a moon or a sun.
And navigating by these small gifts
we march, steeped in a sense of 'us'
walking amongst our descendants
reminding them that the love of one's country
is a currency earned only by the few

until, halted by our burdens
we cut our homes into the earth as best we can;
aware that so much of what we are is reduced
to learning how to stay alive
and knowing the slowest way to die.

Condemned

Time is very limited now.
A notice was attached
to an outer wall
months ago. There are
the usual objectors of course,
but there is very little
left to preserve;
merely a dishevelled shell
that no longer offers
any resistance to the outside.
The strong foundation
was buried too many years ago.

Too little left to remind
of the past; a history
crumbled and forgotten:
rooms filled with people,
parties, a family.
And too little left
to reflect on the crime
committed years earlier,
or to care
about the lethal injection
to be administered at 5 a.m.
the next morning.

Echo

Every night I lean over towards you
and steal for myself one final glance
as I turn out the lamp.

The palsied light frames you in silver
confidently striding forward
intimidating your own smile.

You're caught in a pea-souper
and only occasionally encountered;
a kind of vision that quickens and fades

to an impression, searching sleep,
navigating its way along the borders;
like the limit to one's vocabulary

with a clarity of oversight
not easily understood from a distance
of vertebrate to invertebrate.

I know what it is that you're thinking
as you fidget with that last
ten pound note in your pocket:

of the wavering horizons of youth
and all its inherent glow
in a land where optimism

almost disappears into perspective
and hands clutching at the new materialism
try to hide the threads of a worn world.

On the death of the past

there will be momentary mourning.
Even as people come out of their houses
to question themselves, and each other
the streets will be lit with expressions of the minute
reflecting instead the day's empty shine.
Entering forever the Modern Era
a time that no longer knows when it is,
where history has never been.
Ancestors can't inform their descendants;
the elderly will be looked upon with puzzlement.
Stonehenge will become contemporary art
and ammonites pretty ornaments.
People will be born with the conviction
that one moment is like every other,
and move between them
with all the speed of electricity;
without glimpsing the horizons of their language:
the tongue will no longer taste words
like tradition, veteran, or antiquity
and all that was ever written by Plato,
or Shakespeare, will be written today;
because experience is extinct, and insight is instinct
the days will see the world merely as it is
within the palling echoes of their lineage.

An equation and a final solution

$$T = \sum_{i=1}^{t=100} \frac{(2rFV)}{[Y^2]} + [n_c] \sum^{T_d=8000} - e = 800\,000$$

Where:

T	=	total killed after 100 days
i	=	dummy index
t	=	time (days)
Y	=	a constant
r	=	reactant mixture
F	=	force
V	=	velocity
n_c	=	political indecision (a constant)
C	=	electric charge
S	=	entropy (measure of disorder)
T_d	=	subtotal killed per day
e	=	equilibrium

Rwanda, 1994

Forensics

Trees draw into the sky's sudden contraction.
Instinct fills a small clearing that will become habitat,
leaving us silenced by what we didn't see.
                              And now,
there's a jumbled archipelago
that hangs from the ground, showing in abstract
the anatomy of this incident:
the sudden snap of nerve;
the sudden deviation from form and structure,
until complexity became simplicity;
the only signature of violence within all distance.
                    Grass begins to lengthen;
the air cooling to its present tense.
Its tracks have been caught in the sun
and have dried through the day.

Unnatural histories

The dodo had its time cut short
By porcine pests and sailors' sport

A worldwide love of ivory
Brought elephants catastrophe

The loggers cleared as thylacines
Succumbed to hunting and disease

Captured, caged and packed in crates
Auks filled boats as lobster bait

On desert plains an ancient birth:
A primate stood and changed the earth

Chromosome

x marks the spot. where we begin being us. a pinpoint of light. signature of an unknown. the unknown in the equation. inverted commas enclosing quotations around a double entendre. suffix and prefix personified. twist in every turn. crick in every neck. as we struggle to follow the strand of conversation. question: answer: question: answer. for every x there's a why. talking in code. in uppercase. a bit more than binary. dyslexia decoded in chain reaction. multiplied and multiplied. becoming the well-read the unread and the unreadable. a crucifix in rotation. the crux of any matter. criss-crossing and crossing over until we're outed. our coda decoded. misspelling followed by a downward spiral to crucifixion. a genetic double fault. the greatest double-cross: truths swapped with half-truths. identity divided into its other selves. a tiny birth. the softest of big bangs. moving along the information superhighway. linking and defining generations.

Form and function

Ignore what the scientists say. Fingernails
are for making long, slow strokes along a naked thigh
for orbiting the dimples of Venus
for etching a name in a lover's back.

They're for tracing the perfect angle of a child's nose
the story held in the veins of a leaf
the soft shapes of clouds. They're for tracing
the paths that form the constellations.

Occasionally they're nibs for writing on the air
full stops for pointed remarks
pivot points for cartwheels. They're canvases
transmitting a deeper colour, within.

But if you're talking to a scientist, and you're asked
                              just call them
peculiar modifications of the epidermis, and say
they're for protecting the distal phalanges.

To *Aliceathrips palmeri*

Think of this
    as a letter of introduction.
We're not related, and you don't know me, but I know
that you're carried on the hot winds
that you've lived in the long grass,
for how many summers?
I too lived in Alice Springs for several years
but wouldn't call myself native.
We couldn't be less alike;
    there's you, fully winged,
with a yellow body and eight-segmented antennae;
and me, somewhat overweight, with brown hair and psoriasis.
And I only have two legs, neither of which bears spines.
And you're so small (although others of my kind
have no doubt thought of me in this way).
How it must be,
    to bear a name from another species.
Surely each of you is as different as I am
to my neighbours, or siblings.
Such names are often bestowed
on the microscopic, the many-legged, the moist
and yet,
    to discover just what isn't in a name:
how you sense the world; to learn your language.
Although I regret your misnomer – what else are you now
but a sign that says indirectly that *I* was here –
    to *Scaptia beyonceae*,
Aptostichus angelinajolieae, and *Orsonwelles macbeth*
I sincerely apologise.

Growing notes for banksias

1

A book says the one called Wallum
grows as a small, gnarled, twisted tree
under more favourable conditions.

2

The eminent naturalist whose name you bear
likened the country to the back of a lean cow.
You helped give Botany Bay its name.

3

Even as a young plant
the Old Man Banksia
resembles an old man.

4

Giant Candles, illuminating the south-west.

5

They say your leaves are alternate, sometimes whorled
that your dense inflorescence is subtended by a bract.
And your cotyledons have acute basal auricles.

6

Generations have made a sweet liquor of your flowers.
I look on your muted struggle and drink.

7

The wind burnishes your grain
the sun burns you into being
and your being is burned into artefact.
Tourists know you as coasters and pencil holders
ornaments and photo frames.
Small eyes are glued just above yawning follicles
that speak of centuries.

8

You broke the desolation of King George Sound;
became the clouds the explorer Eyre never saw.

9

Your passive smoking is nothing less than addiction
and every year your seeds disappear into blackness.
Jumping spiders fill the spaces like confessionals;
(many are the sins of an ambush predator).

10

Eucalyptus and melaleuca are your associates
but dryandra is the voice that was always in your head.

11

Clinging to the coast as if watered by the sea
some of the largest I've seen
line the land's edge
framing old age and unacred silence
elemental changes in the light.
You define a continent
in the shape of Australia.

The poplar effect

The landscape slows its
diurnal trade, offering
finally a gift
before the day withdraws the
outer limits of its reach.

Beginning now, the
listing afternoon sends up
a flare, rising
from the shadowing suburbs
breaching sunset's silent arc.

Ten thousand tiny
flags arranged exactly, like
overlapping tiles
or soldiers from some foreign
nation. The sky flickers a

newly minted name
as alternating colours
arrive in couplets
on the air. And when I move
toward and untoward, the

lighting shifts to where
it never was: refracted
and combined until
nature flies a fluttering
lie. As if attempting to

break this connection
of sight and self, neighbouring
cockatoos loop, then
wheel around, hiccuping their
approach with a snappy show

of overstatement;
a clockwork snail resolves
to better itself;
while this crowded summer,
as fluent and transient

as the aurora
or an eclipse, underplays
its rhythm, waving
quietly in approval
like some royal passer-by.

Mayfly

no longer green around the gills
he is unsheathed from adolescence

four-oared and paddling the airwaves
in a kind of semaphore, his present tense

is part Icarus and part Romeo
blindly conforming in a blizzard of silent fervour –

confetti to choke the throats of animals
and smooth the tread of tyres –

until the complicit gesturing of time
and cosmic forces skew his balance and weight

his movements; a muddle of spirals
and spins that exposes nature's counterfeit

as merely a scent, drifting in earthly currents
betraying all in his nothingness

Nomenclature

The Western quoll is as long as a school ruler
from nose to rump; add another for its tail.
Eats nothing that doesn't move.
So named because the ethnographer Joseph Banks
transcribed the Guugu Yimidhirr word *dhigul*
as *Je-Quoll*; and because it never occurred east
of the Dividing Range.
Also known as *Dasyurus geoffroii*
meaning hairy tailed French zoologist
chuditch, *kuninka*, wild cat
in central Australia it's called *atyelpe* by the Arrernte people
giving its name to an important totem.
Eating it was forbidden
except for the elderly wild cat men
who last tasted it in the 1950s.
The early whitefellas of Alice Springs were not so adept
at the correct pronunciation of Arrernte
and all that remains here
      is Achilpa Street
pointing to its last refuge
two thousand kilometres in the distance, the sign
as long as a school ruler.

Weeding

These aliens
that arise so quickly

by spontaneous generation.
I pull each one up by the hair

and feel its struggle
in the wind.

But they have a right to be here
as much as anything else,

and they have come here
by their own means, these migrants

looking for greener pastures.
All they want is their chance

to sow their seed –
like the rest of us.

But I'm committing systematic herbicide
to achieve monocultures

of edible reds, yellows
and greens.

I am a willing participant
in their extinction –

at least on my soil.

Meanwhile, at Floriade…

I

The parade is assembled and laid out before us
      beginning with the magnolia,
the first of the flowering kind.
Next, irises attract males of many species
      while pansies are deflowered
at the sight of a eucalypt, the floral emblem
of everywhere.
      The dandelion's here, uninvited,
entering itself in all the competitions.
An ambulance pauses at the sickly jonquils,
      while violas play to the crowd
with each at risk of being snipped at the ankles.
      Another favourite, the tulip,
seduces a man while he wonders how the naked lady
got its name. The audience stands and applauds;
      caught up in it all
a young woman nosedives into its stamens.

II

Magnolia
Simple say the botanists, with too many parts
for 'loves me, loves me not'.

Tulips
Any subtlety of perfume lost in erect colour.
Goblets of the finest red.

Irises
Not quite bruising; leaning in optimism –
the vase half full.

Prickly pear
Undone by a moth while meditating on the self
as desert.

Wattle
Birds swim in kilos of yellow, spreading its seed;
so much fluff and snow.

Daffodils
An argument won by image over substance.
Trumpeting yellow! I am here!

Wisteria
Grows like it sounds, Medusa crimped as a bride.
A confetti of petals.

Dandelion
Shares a bed with grass. Alight in the shadows
of people.

Monday, 8 a.m.

Breakfast was tasty, but hardly a distraction.
Bathed in the future tense
he turns the ignition and tunes into FM everything
slipping beneath the waves until it feels like a Friday.
Ahead of him, the walls are clean and white.
Paper shredders are warming up
as the first of the morning conversations fill the rooms:
finely honed stories of weekend inactivities;
recalling the day when that new guy on level two
got lost in a process and was never found.
A freshly brewed rumour permeates the air.
In room 101, artists are already stroking canvasses,
facilitators are facilitating, drafting a submission
proposing a business case requesting
an executive summary to get signed off.
A moment of irony passes, unobserved
while the sign outside says
'No entry – emergency in progress.'
Floorwalkers drift through corridors;
prefects look with fresh eyes
at the junior staff, who are all dressed up
to receive their dressing down
as the adjacent car park performs its roll call.
They've come from across the suburbs
to do all they can for the department.
He pulls in, half hoping something has been forgotten,
half thinking. What was it his wife said?
We are made of what we make.
Seeing the day unfold in front of him
he walks through concrete, bitumen, glass
and enters the grey and the cold and the grey.

A lesson in servitude

We're stranded between morning teas
until a young prole is found out
trying to hide his birthday;
he comes back to a desk full of balloons, cake
and a print out of the Social Function Guidelines.
As the last of the crumbs are pecked away
a prefect spins like a neutron star
talking of how best to get to an irrelevant destination
and I'm in a landing craft on the way to Omaha.
She asks me what I think, when it doesn't matter
what I think. But it wasn't always like this.
It's not what you were, she laughs
it's what you are now.

Capital cities

Canberra avian, composed, two-pieced, two-wheeled *Sydney* pacemaker, opaque, original, indifferent *Melbourne* caffeinated, lop-sided, seasoned, black *Hobart* linear, familial, straddled, connected *Adelaide* radial, vanilla, viticultural, piggy-in-the-middle *Perth* mediterranean, resourceful, secluded, sparkling *Darwin* isothermal, regenerated, momentary, evolutionary *Brisbane* warm, wooden, meandering, six-legged

At the corner store

As I offer her
my small change
and a few smaller words

I notice the shop assistant
is wearing a necklace
of love bites

which embellish
and blemish
her skin.

Perhaps a multicoloured sign
warning people
to stay away.

Or a set
of traffic lights:
her demeanour softening

as they change
from red to amber to green –
'Do you want a bag?'

William Carlos Williams

wrote as if
everything
he observed
occurred

in

slow

motion

Thank you for your submission

thank you for the opportunity to consider it
very sorry to have kept these so long
please accept our apologies for the delay
I normally reply within 12 months
regretfully, I am unable to place your poem
I'm afraid we haven't used them
we are unable to use the enclosed material
we receive a very large number
all of which are refereed blind
many of them of very high quality
yours haven't been selected
it's impossible to reply more specifically
it's either too obvious or too obscure
lines 5–6 let it down
it's a bit too long
it isn't right for us
it isn't what we're looking for
it wouldn't fit with our editorial policy
it wouldn't 'fit', if you know what I mean
please submit again in the future
we look forward to reading future submissions
I encourage you to continue to submit your poems
unfortunately, the next issue is full
there is no more space for the next 12 months
there is definitely no space in the coming year to publish your work
good luck with your writing

Untitled

You remarked that poets are most obsessed with pain
    and it's true
how I like to jab and dart, poke and pinch
    my way across the page.
Today I compose my greatest work,
    a kaleidoscopic portrait of the self
in high definition,
    uninhibited by a truth that guides
most practitioners of our craft.
    The surreal and the subterranean
are mixed with newly planed subject-verb splits
    highly sharpened sentence-closers
and as I lunge in a final, dazzling, triumphant strike
    I fall to the floor
killed by my own poem.

Notes

In my mother's country: *ayepe-arenye* – the Arrernte word for a type of caterpillar that lives on the tar vine (*Boerhavia* species). The caterpillar is one of the main dreamings for the Alice Springs area. Source: J. Henderson and V. Dobson (1994), *Eastern and Central Arrernte to English Dictionary*, Institute for Aboriginal Development, Alice Springs. The caterpillar is the immature stage of the hawk moth *Hyles livornicoides*, a local native species.

A western shade of red: the phrase 'whispered in Alice's ear' is paraphrased from a passage in *Through the Looking Glass, and what Alice found there*, by Lewis Carroll (1871).

Extract from a record of an expedition through central Australia: *alatja* – a visitor; one who has just left or has only just arrived; *yimpi* – a butterfly chrysalis; both from the Pintupi/Luritja dialects of the Western Desert. Source: K.C. & L.E. Hansen (1992), *Pintupi/Luritja Dictionary*, 3rd edition, Institute for Aboriginal Development, Alice Springs. Lines 10–14 are paraphrased from the writings of William Dampier, extracted from CSIRO (1991) *The Insects of Australia*, (2nd edition). CSIRO, Melbourne University Press, p. 225.

At Emily Gap: *altyerrenge* = the Dreaming, or Dreamtime; from the Arrernte language of central Australia. Source: J. Henderson & V. Dobson (1994), *Eastern and Central Arrernte to English Dictionary*, Institute for Aboriginal Development Press, Alice Springs.

Naturam primum cognoscere rerum: Latin, translates as 'First to learn the nature of things'. It is the motto of the Australian National University.

Convicts sentenced at Norfolk Island & Port Arthur, Tasmania: Source material from the Tasmanian Archive and Heritage Office, and R. Lord (1995), *The Isle of the Dead, Port Arthur*, 4th edition, Richard Lord & Partners, Taroona, Tasmania.

Echo: the phrase 'wavering horizons of youth and all its inherent glow' is paraphrased from the poem 'The Aurora Australis' by Mary Hannay Foott, extracted from *Where the Pelican Builds and other poems* (1885), Gordon & Gotch, Brisbane.

Form and function: part of the scientific definition and function is paraphrased from Wikipedia.

Growing notes for banksias: the book referred to in the first stanza is *A Field Guide to Banksias*, by I. Holliday and G. Watton (1990), 2nd edition, Hamlyn Australia, Melbourne. The second stanza was informed by *The Endeavour Journal of Joseph Banks, 1768–1771*, edited by J.C. Beaglehole (1963), 2nd edition, Angus & Robertson, Sydney. The eighth stanza was informed by *Journals of Expeditions into Central Australia*, (1845), by Edward John Eyre. *Australiana Facsimile Edition No. 7*, (1964), Libraries Board of South Australia, Adelaide.

Nomenclature: *kuninka*, from C. Goddard (1996), *Pitjantjatjara/Yankunytjatjara to English Dictionary*, 2nd edition, Institute for Aboriginal Development Press, Alice Springs. Reference is also made to content in *The Endeavour Journal of Joseph Banks, 1768–1771*, edited by J.C. Beaglehole (1963), 2nd edition, Angus & Robertson, Sydney.

Monday, 8 a.m.: 'room 101' from *Nineteen Eighty-four*, by George Orwell (1949), Martin Secker & Warburg.

A lesson in servitude: 'prole' also from *Nineteen Eighty-four*.

www.ingramcontent.com/pod-product-compliance
Lightning Source LLC
Chambersburg PA
CBHW062159100526
44589CB00014B/1877